I Choose To Love

JEFFREY D. JUBELIRER

Inquiries and Book Orders should be addressed to:

Great Writers Media
Email: info@greatwritersmedia.com
Phone: (302) 918-5570
16192 Coastal Highway, Lewes DE 19958, USA

ISBN: 978-1-960939-34-0 (sc)
ISBN: 978-1-960939-35-7 (ebk)

Contents

I Bow My Head

I bow my head
To a white shining dove.
Love is effective
Above Him my head
We appreciate
And serve an honorable Master.
We sing our songs
You must guess
Rest to the bartender
Rest to the love and
Their birds and buds.

Is It Time the Opportunity of Respect

Is it time the opportunity of Respect
To set the limits,
or walk over the boundary
The May Day celebration
The May Day operation.
We are listening,
Even the ducks will speak
And I wonder while wandering
If we should measure a tree
Or all the trees with their flowers
And the blossoming of creation
Built on love.
We are taking time and still
Giving back to God
And his own.

Maybe Different

A little young lady kneeled to the floor
Reaching for her bag of candy

Turned upside down for prayer
Looking sky high I was there
A face she didn't forget
And the wonder
As I wander when again if ever.
To see a face of love and warmth
I do really like myself
And choose for honor and faith
And trust.
And all along a prodigal son.
No, not the big deal
Maybe someone different

Guess

We are all the Children
brought out on the dark
for the flowing of blood to the Champion
Walking down the road his last days
And the new Champion Praising God.

The Number I Take

Am I deluding myself

For the feeling is so real
As I can capture and count to ten
To pursue further
The course of greatness I need and want
For the heaven I love to feel
For the God I may return his kiss
And I wave to the universe
That doesn't know me
But would be infinitely changed
Had I not come about

Be Friends, the Way

Dearest are friends with me
See the sky bright
Right to the night and day
Wrong or right
Long is the strength
Our feelings
Stay together in spirit
Dancing for each other
Help us make the day
Sing songs.
Cups of coffee close
Tasting, tantalized
No gross error
Send us closer
Smiling at daisies and robes
Sounding out our reception
Charting special reasons
Counting up unity
Following along the day.
May I please have the way today?
The way is having friends.

Nice Smiles Today

Reasoned overlooking destined
Time charts might prove
The points are up
To arts and billions
Air bubbles singing
Forward grabbing on the trees
A Vine Street, Spruce and Pine Streets
Upward trips and changes

We speak to secure and hope
All are accepted
And accept to ease
The pain
Joy might be hidden
Then we will laugh
With justice
On our side
Tremendous times to come.
Trumpets Magnificent sets of threads,
Nice smiles today,
Sunshine or rain
Clearing away the dirt
At gutters
Fixing up party lines.

Friendship on a Long Walk to Heaven

Friendship on a long walk to heaven
Or the place to achieve
And accomplish dreams.
The snake pass was crossed.
There was an invitation of a good day.
Someone caring, to be accepted
One might not know we have
Some wisdom available and strength
To be over, lifting up
Showing growth
And we come open to the wind
Mutual joy.

Ode to Judy

To be now
And the reason,
Entertaining and comfortable
Appreciation
We think to be for all
And all can grow creating
The sky
Already from the beginning
The ode to Judy
Friendship at a smile
Truth at a handshake
Fraternal love eternal
And to our sensitive
And sensible Judy
We pray and wish
For her happiness
And strength
And love
For herself
Feeling Better

Feeling Better

Scented perfume and cologne to please
Attract someone helping the future
To need to purpose not the greed.
Leading and following,
We talk for time
Pray for youth
Thought and thanked
We do grow every day.
Alive
The mountains are climbed
Your choice Welcomed thoughts positive,
The energy bright is a gift to us feeling better.

I Was a Non-Conformist

Going way back
Independent and too strong for my size
Brave and courageous or filled with hutzpah.
Did I go too far away?
Am I coming back?
Who chooses
The conforming decisions
The boundaries where?
Can good always be here?
Valuable decisions,
Valuable evaluations,
Valuable results,
I am no loser.
I relax and realize the gifts of a brain
And I can care
And love also,
I think I can.

Home Protection

Coming and going until the new place
The home protection
The clear reflection Peace and joy,
Fulfillment thus touched
Within my soul.

All around a climactic setting
Strength is for an outside world
Forgive me whom I did hurt
I did try to do well
Respectful and respectable
Forgetting hurt on orders to forgive.

Prayers get answered sometimes
Some ways being thankful;
Youth and joy,
Caring and knowing
Love might be possible
Residing onward upward.

Sometimes Later Into Night

Sometimes later into night
Maybe on early time
To be with me
In my heart
And mind
And soul Peace coming.
Joy and feeling good
To accomplish
Alone but maybe not forgetting
Chosen and fire
Called Anointed
Presented And developing
Each moment. I'm kind love to myself,
A failure, and I
I myself
And should try to give when asked
With no fears.
Please give me courage.

For Both

Living, loving, creating.
There is time and responsibility
Give eternal bliss with knowledge.
We can start, and we can stop
Reacting together for each other
To the return;
Two souls separate
Two souls united,
Grabbing gentle the thoughts, grasping hearts
Are essence and stable hope,
Days to days
Rays of the sun and glare, fair moonlight
Take our turns famously
Rewarding and for both

God Helps

Smiling as taking the distance,
We do not disturb.
Close your eyes
To give complete time
For the sight or foresight
Smiling and rubbing skin.
Until contentment touches
Riding up the hill It must be rightful, guaranteed.
Smiling and giving the kiss
While warming the heart
Making me get up
To be strong,
That's our type of poetry.
Live, learn
Giving God our pain
He loves us
And will help.

Prepare

One candle at a time
holding a first wish for love
we moved on and gentle giving
all the emotion
and alone with all or some.
We welcome newness,
and courageous strength
warmed still here a new place,
a new day seeking laughter and joy.
Rekindle the light remaining,
small candles for past and future,
lights for the present of life
enduring soon to be one at all call.
Holy Spirit welcome,
The Lord knows and best is alive day
and night preparing to be.

Perfect together

Excellent in the making
Straight to the ends
And fortunate for the soft touch
The relation of kindness
Coming more and more
To look at sweet legs
And soft, soft lips
Smooth
My "baby love" is supreme I dream
Cutting the grass Keeping it real green;
Fruitful trees flowing while the roads are all safe.
Automatic joy as my heart finds pretty
And intelligent spices.
Truth analyzing all gracefully
Or a little obsessive.
We could be perfect together.

Heaven All Around

We are smiling today more than yesterday
A thank you goes to you
Dear Jesus rolling in the tide.
So fresh and clean
Growing winds and sensitive friends
We have acceptance of life.
This very moment and day
We must be the best way
A now focus is true time
Open and willing
Prepared
Open eyes for which is onto more
The way shares
To care and be thankful,
With the moon and sun
The stars are all a portion
Of heaven all around
Positively being.

Stings Were Plucked

Strings were plucked
As my emotions let out
All the different sounds of music
I am sitting down on a lap
A harp being plucked
By the Lord perhaps
I hold my head too high
Perhaps I hold my head too high
There is something alive
And honest.
I too am alive with all the emotions
Singing and praying to the Lord;
And the harp of an angel
Sings and prays too.
Never wanting my soul ended.
Each chord as played is my each
Moment of heart.
I reach to you.
The angels play the harp
Melody from my God.

I Am Looking In the Other Room

I am looking in the other room
Heaven on earth
The attitude, clean and always
Striving to be good
And you promise a mansion in heaven
Lord, thank you for your mercy.
Did I read the poem?
Are you missing me?
Jesus Christ, "Are you Emmanuel?"
Please don't let me be sacrilegious
And my wife and I do sanctify each other.
That is what we were told.

Active Grace

Such pleasure and necessity
we read and learn I take joy.
True life of grace I can somehow recall
tendered words and thoughts growing.
Hope turns into faith holiness
becomes and born to be coming.
We forgive
we receive
we give favor in the moment.
And all is remembered that to mind,
mood to render our work is found and finished.

A Place Called Home

Sweet sweat
Grasping further, faster, deeper
I kissed the night
The moon gives me victory
And glory till all
Around too much seasons and days
Then God for life and children
And women who want to love me
Respectfully.
Trust can happen
When and where
The sunshine alive
The purple robe I saved for
Heaven Cherish me trying not to demand
And special people
Relating spiritually
Speaking in many tongues
My wife, she is wandering
In a place called
Home

The Staff Arose So High

The staff arose so high
The clouds began to cleanse the earth
Charming charmed together.

I knew I could live and be
With a higher power of love
Sitting quickly amidst problems but flowers,

More flowers grew as the problems were
Outwitted with smiles
Our sky is clearing moving the strong.

Sunshine

Sunshine Rhyme my rhythm
Teach me someone today I can care
Feel energy
Grow and carry
Fulfillment of love where
How and why
The cunning ability
With pockets filled with bread
Talking to God
A sincere thank you
Given life and time
To think
To run
Walk with spirit
And consideration and appreciation
Really a need for being appreciated.

Sweet Smell of the Success

Sweet smell of the success
That lies ahead of us through the Lord
He approaches my heart and mind now and forever
With you being tender and together
yielding to your awareness of
Home and striving for what is righteous,
We hold our hands high together

To the light of the cross
And recognize our trust and necessity in its power
We must put behind our mistakes and learn together
For we are starting to climb a mountain
With a lake of calm pure water
And lots of sunshine Creating smiles
We two together
Will bring to warm the heart of God.
We hope and believe

Welcome to My Paradise

Welcome to my paradise, dear lady
Welcome to a place of peace.
Hold my hand,
Touch my head to dream.
Close your eyes,
Lay down,
Stretch out your past
Presently forget the search.
You are here
Sound never ending, to good.
We will relax
Together remaining
Softly independent
Whoosh of the water coming
Almost to our hearts.
We stand and yet are placed in ground,
Sand melting our positions
As water flows to an innermost source
The moon glows asking our names.
Our minds wander to music seldom heard.
We don't need to wish.

The ocean in and we close to heaven.
We forget taking on a foundation,
Part of the whole creation,
Any piece of pie appreciated.

I Service Tenderness

Sincerely I service tenderness
Away from anger
Bitterness overcome
And welcomed springtime
With budding flowers
As we close our eyes together.
You dream I rest
Comfortable and
Carrying us away
From Hell.

Tonight To Thanks

Dear you I realize your ultimate class
Possible tonight
Across the table with a candle
Glowing silent profile
Holding all
Your hand and a sigh
Dreams of your voice
Speaking prayers
For my soul awake
Tonight as we drift into peace together.
Tomorrow the sun will come up
An eternal universal smile of thanks.

I Stopped, Halted, Looked

I stopped, halted, looked
In a window
Thanked God for the time
Relaxed on two feet
Thought about the evening
Throwing myself into inner parts.
There was a room awaiting me
Holding my very breath
A hug, a whisper, a kiss
The conversation uplifting
Maybe a poem
And resting in the love, the peace.
What I could do
Who I could serve
When I could talk
Love just might continue.
I do!

Don't Ask, Don't Tell

Don't ask, don't tell
Sweetly, hardly lighten the fear.
Close eyes and smile,
And that might be all.
But then again maybe just enough
With mercy and justice
And lots of thanks
For humility and the right time.

Tenderly We Entered Our Eyes

Tenderly we entered our eyes
One last glimpse until tomorrow
Knowing we held tonight
We liked the opportunity to touch
We saw as moments
We loved till right now
Natural and accepted
Truth and honor becoming powerful
Seeking what can be found
To build a friendship
Allowed to be free
And prayers for protection.
We must be thankful for all this,
Calm to develop
And let myself be holding, reaching
Out Times to learn deep
To the soul And the need.

Dazed, Dazzled

Crazy about your "you"
And you still say you love me
While I talk and listen
Glistening lights out of my eyes
Deep into the soul
Coal turning into diamond mines
Rhymes telling songs
To come out of my head
Asking, telling at time
You require
The knowing and real showing
Activity around
And awarded
The seas seized for peace
And energy active
Simultaneous
Up and above
Down and cursing
Momentary lapse
Forgiveness and grace
Tell your story.

And Believed

A great pleasure
In this world
My places
Reach the moment.
Giving a smile
Warming with warmth
And pleasure gives
Someone
Near, close
And believed
To be heavenly
Touched.

Sweet and True I Thought You Were

Sweet and true I thought you were
Tell me why the sunshine is high
Tell me will I always cry
Tell me why.
Sigh and then realize ties remain
Lies are gone
Perpetuate the seasons
Reasons to hold on
Going forward
Asking today
And a strong day
We shared
We cared
Moving along if I can
Sleep much
Such I do
Much I feel
You were someone who says "Loving is for us"
You and me

I Hope and Splendor

To dream tonight of you
Would be necessary,
I need you every day.
To draw closer to your love
Lying awake and hoping
That tomorrow you will
Call for me, I hope in splendor.
Our growing eyes together
Make for special
Days and nights
To live and reach
Together.

Memories Come

Memories come to my mind
A heart to think you are dreams I always reached
But could not unite
In heaven.
You are my friend
God taught me to care for you
As I hear you sing. The emotion creates so much warmth
On this cold day
And tenderness please touch
My words to give
Your ears my love.
My love Turning on and carrying
While being carried Memories come.

Dear Highness

Dear highness
Dear grass and trees
And how many will love me
Warm and close
Speak to me your love
And statements
For the good and
Do we watch
The news anymore,
Sometimes to blast the
Radio with high
Level of pleasure
Same and sober
And looking to all sides.

Petal of All Flowers

We are all petals of all flowers
Growing together in hopes
Of love Each one expressive
Till the completion of the garden
Welcomes and graciously
Smiles really
Though often sweated for
The ground solidly remains
Though changes
And is cleaned.

Seeing the Bright

Super time
Supper time with springs
Of water fresh, Place a guest of honor.
A goal works Treating myself for love
And glory just enough. Stuffing feathers of doves
All around me See the bright
Completely Gaining accessibility.
In the minds Open and willing
I receive from much. I thank all those who believe
And can overlook
The flowers which die.

Beyond the Sunlight

Beyond the sunlight in hopes
And prayers Singing a song of love to those
And theirs Give me some work
And a heavenly clerk
Over moons and stars
In trains searching
California
And all over the Rio Grande
Mostly through the time
In the church Of Philadelphia
And spreading words Peace and harmony
And throwing away any anger
Cleaning up and clearing
With space
And friendship

Wandering

Wandering
And resting on the greener
Grass
Shield
The freedom.
Recovery of life
To be
And I must watch "Where" and "who".
I know "what"
And "why".
Principles come to me
Pleasurably
Over and out
And in for relief.
Tender times talk tomorrow
Or just "Today".

To Each and Owning

To each and owning,
She is and she was and I will
Love forever.
The words are here and there are many
Times to love, to think
And maybe more at the end of the rainbow, which shines for all,
And ask for guidance of God's will.
Accept his decision with grateful hope
And thanksgiving, I believe.

Tingling On Love Time

Tingling on love time
Singing the songs
I love
Each day hold close
Warming a heart
But never too soon.
A few touches
And superior
Integrity Wash clean
Another day
Forever

Attempt

My mirror gets closer at this time
Whispering "Take me in your heart".
Flowers blossoming
Around the borders
See me where my heart now pumps,
Further the race for the powers of sight
Resist in action
Not just talking.
Getting away from the devil
Trying to be goodness,
God works through me
And wants me to be good.

Open

Sincerely my open heart has waited till now
To open together with another heart,
Open to my heart. I write but would rather look
Into the eyes my Lord has allowed
For me to stare at eternally.
And I say thank you Jesus
Thank you god
Thank you Sherry.

My Heart Belongs to You and Jesus

My heart belongs to you and Jesus,
As we touch in the starlight of our coming desire
Hold my hand and smile.
Speak your beautiful voice in song and praise.
You are my Sherry,
My dream of long life
And fruit and permanence toward
Heaven's open door
Kiss me for a moment to last eternally
To close our eyes together and open
Our eyes to a better tomorrow
Faith, hope, and love-my blessings
Kindly water the flowers
And keep them always Growing at our life
Together united and seen for good

And God Created Us Cells of Life

And God created us cells of life
And keep on rolling the pizza dough
Or bagels or doughnuts
Or Pepperidge Farm delight's
Or just plain Wonder bread
Falling down from heaven
Rising upwards
The sky and the earth or choice.
Lights made, lights burning
Candles glowing,
Showing medicine for almost anything
Tripping over feet in the dark
Room alone and getting called for light.
Thunder and lightening
Exciting also to be with
More than something.

Best of New and Old

To have a kiss goodnight
The lady was tonight
Smiling
Caressing this pointed heart
Sweated palms
A man reaching and letting go
For her soft excitement
Composure of dining
Ready for kindness for sighs
And grasping sight,
The petals before they break
The original flowers
Sweet of my rhyme
Dined to the time
Carrying together the threshold of light
And permanent gratitude.
We have seen the flowers and smelling
With our eyes closed
With promises of sense.
Aroused, arriving New birth
Yet retaining experience.

Late Night

Lamps on to lateness of night
Knighthood special
Wonderful normal being in the tune
And going for the sun working any time.
Resting or arresting the condition.
Coming a little late but still,
And sitting quiet
Peaceful mind praising
Or maybe a look for flowers
A rose, a daisy will die or be remembered
Importantly granted a forward motion
To attract emotion with a song
A dance A kiss long waited
Exciting day into the night.

Remembering

In the dreams
They come true or real
Just seeing another love from long ago
Yesterday gone
Alone physically
Times tough
Painting on a window
And the window is open to see the feelings
All alone to let the pain go forward
And snatched.
Colors even in the shadow.
The light is up high
Kisses honorable
Remembering love and dancing even more,
The shore glowed but now
I stay home
To keep writing until a sleepy time.

This is the Man in Line

This is the man in line
For first love Heart pounding
Words speaking
Bathing in spirit
I walk out and enter the garden
With arms full of flowers
That last with pure water and we.

My Beautiful Wife

My beautiful wife
My beautiful wife
Life God gave us
Touched the service of yeshua
I look there or definitely
Here
At my wife
Loving me enough to face the world
We as one home
Knowing first before or on the way
Maybe infinity
We can all come together
Our sameness and our peculiarity
Giving completeness
Originally to be from the beginning
To on for the future forever.

www.ingramcontent.com/pod-product-compliance
Lightning Source LLC
Chambersburg PA
CBHW020921140626
46545CB00015B/1158